STOP SMOKING

The Essential Guide

Simon
Daubney

Stop Smoking – The Essential Guide is also available in accessible formats for people with any degree of visual impairment. The large print edition and eBook (with accessibility features enabled) are available from Need2Know. Please let us know if there are any special features you require and we will do our best to accommodate your needs.

First published in Great Britain in 2011 by
Need2Know
Remus House
Coltsfoot Drive
Peterborough
PE2 9BF
Telephone 01733 898103
Fax 01733 313524
www.need2knowbooks.co.uk

Contents

Introduction

For some people, stopping smoking is one of the hardest things they've ever tried to do.

You may have tried several times in the past and relied on different methods to do it.

The aim of this book is to help you to look at what you did well and give you tips on how to improve on your previous successes. It is designed to be thought-provoking and interactive in its approach, so that you can find ways of changing how you feel about tobacco to a point where it becomes easier to say no to it and be free.

Contained within its pages is information to guide and inform, along with interactive elements that will inspire you to be creative and make stopping smoking as easy as possible.

The more you understand your addiction the better, so this guide takes you through all the stages; from understanding your addiction, to deciding why it is best to stop, (for yourself), the benefits you can expect, some thoughts on addictive thinking and some traps and triggers along the way, and how to avoid them.

The right answers can only come from you. We are all different, and how you relate to your addiction will be just as unique.

Smoking is one of strongest addictions known to Man, with heroin addicts even reporting it being harder to give up nicotine than heroin.

I have seen many people make life hard for themselves, and the idea of this book is to give a few tips to help make it easier. It does not give all the answers, but it is a book of information and tips given by someone who used to be a smoker and now helps people to stop.

I wish you well on your journey to stopping smoking, and if you remember nothing else, when you make changes, make them as much fun as possible. If they are an improvement then the new routines become comfortable quickly.

'When you make changes, make them as much fun as possible.'

Disclaimer

This book gives general information only. The information regarding health issues, medications and what is available is also general information. It does not replace the role of your NHS Stop Smoking service advisors, GP, or any other medical staff that help you with your health. If you have any concerns you should contact these people for help and advice.

Chapter One

Defining Tobacco Addiction

What is addiction?

In this chapter, we look at the principle of addiction and when people are ready for a change:

* The addictive nature of smoking.
* Why it is difficult to stop smoking.
* The effects of tobacco use in our lives.

There is a lot of information here that has been included to give an understanding of the addiction, but also to help you with the decisions you need to make to overcome the hold tobacco has over you.

First, how did tobacco get to be so much part of our culture?

The history of smoking

It is widely believed that Sir Walter Raleigh introduced tobacco to England in Elizabethan times. However, it actually arrived a few years earlier, but was made fashionable in rich circles and the queen's court by Sir Walter.

At the end of the 19th century, Phillip Morris discovered a way to mass produce cigarettes. Up until then, tobacco was mainly used only by rich people in society.

The First World War saw cigarettes given in large rations, free of charge, to service personnel who took smoking to home to all classes.

By the Second World War, more people were smoking than ever before, and cigarettes were used as an appetite suppressant. This helped when food was rationed.

By the middle of the 20th century about 80% of the adult population in the UK were smokers. Similar rates were found elsewhere, making it a very normal thing to smoke.

In the summer of 2007 hefty fines were introduced as England went smoke-free. Other parts of the UK had either already become smoke-free or followed suit soon after.

A survey compiled in 2004 showed that support for smoking restrictions in public places was high with 91% of adults favouring restrictions on restaurants, 86% at work and 65% in pubs. Surprising when you think that many of those people questioned were themselves smokers. (General Household Survey 2004. Office for National Statistics, Copyright© 2006, The Information Centre, Lifestyles Statistics. All rights reserved, wwwic.nhs.uk)

The addictive nature of smoking

Who smokes?

About 22% of the population smoke and sadly it's increasing amongst young people and women. In the 1950s it was nearer that figure who did not smoke so there has been very much a reverse in the smoking statistics over the last 60 years.

In fact, in 2004, it was said that over half the current adult population at that time, (52%) had never smoked. (General Household Survey 2004. Office for National Statistics, Copyright© 2006, The Information Centre, Lifestyles Statistics. All rights reserved, wwwic.nhs.uk)

What makes people so dependent on tobacco?

There are three aspects to tobacco/nicotine addiction:

- Smoking is a behavioural dependence. You may see tobacco as something that helps you in your day-to-day life, something that helps with stress or boredom. If you are young, you may feel it makes you look more adult.

- There is a physical need for nicotine as well and smokers without even thinking will naturally adjust their nicotine intake to their normal daily average. That is why if you go on a long-haul flight you may find your pattern changing and you smoke more than you normally would immediately before getting on the plane and immediately on arriving. When the workplace became smoke-free you may have found that you had an extra cigarette in the morning and caught up on the others through the evening.

- Smoking, rather than being a habit, is actually part of your daily rituals and routines, making patterns difficult to break when smoking stops.

Addiction = How you think cigarettes help + your physical need + how your daily routines feel strange without the substance.

The Smoking Triangle

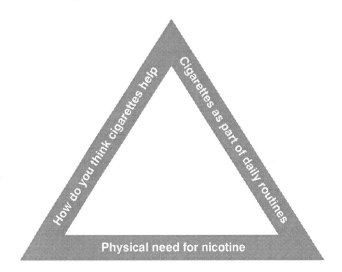

The triangle of tobacco addiction

Other factors regarding the addictive effects of smoking

- The nicotine 'hit' happens within 7 to 15 seconds of puffing on a cigarette when it reaches the brain. This fast action is quicker than most intravenous drugs.

- This speed of action gives feelings of pleasure, arousal and reduced anxiety (although it may be that the anxiety is partly due to being addicted to nicotine in the first place).

- In the short-term this increases the heart rate and blood pressure as nicotine is a stimulant, (despite its reputation for being a relaxant). People mistake this for an excited feeling, (a 'high').

- Long-term smokers develop a tolerance to these effects and need to grow more nicotine receptors to maintain the same level of 'high' that they used to get, which is why you may start off as a three-a-day smoker and end up a 20-a-day smoker before you realise.

Who wants to stop smoking?

There is hope and it starts with wanting to stop.

Many people don't stop first time, and they may try a few times before they manage to succeed.

About 50% of people who attend Stop Smoking services run by the NHS do succeed.

Facts and figures:

- In a household survey in 2004, 80% of smokers had attempted to stop smoking at least once in recent years.
- 72% of smokers reported they wanted to stop smoking.
- When asked about the previous year, 58% of smokers said that they had tried at least once and 22% reported three or more attempts.

(General Household Survey 2004. Office for National Statistics. 2006. www.ic.nhs.uk).

Out of 1,000 smokers aged 20 years old it is estimated that:

- One will be murdered.
- Six will die in motor accidents.
- 250 will die in middle age from smoking.
- 250 will die in old age from smoking.

(Smoking kills, Doh. 1998).

Now would be a good time to start listing all the reasons why you wish to stop smoking in preparation for the planning stage of this book.

Smoking and health issues:

Smoking is the largest preventable cause of death and related diseases and disabilities in the UK.

Which health problems are caused by smoking?

- Cancer of the mouth, oesophagus, lungs, stomach, throat, larynx, blood (leukaemia), kidney, bladder and intestines.
- Chronic obstructive pulmonary disorder, (COPD), or emphysema and other lung problems, including making asthma worse. About 85% of deaths from lung disease are caused by smoking.
- Strokes and poor circulation throughout the body.
- Blood clots.
- Heart disease.
- Osteoporosis, as smoking reduces bone growth and regrowth and therefore slows down the bone repair process. Smoking also makes conditions such as rheumatoid arthritis and osteoarthritis worse.
- Smoking reduces immunity and increases the chances of getting some infections.
- Infertility.
- Smoking can increase the risk of problems in patients with conditions such as diabetes.
- Smoking can interfere with and reduce the effects of some medications such as antidepressants, psychiatric medication, asthma medication, heart and diabetes drugs, some drugs used for respiratory problems and painkillers.
- Smoking raises bad cholesterol types and reduces good cholesterol.

As well as causing some of these illnesses, smoking can slow also down their treatments, making them less effective.

This is by no means all the effects of smoking, and you will notice it is not just the fatal conditions that are an issue here, but also that smoking causes and impairs the treatment of many short and long-term disabilities.

Environmental tobacco smoke

How others are affected by smoking

- Several hundred people die every year from what used to be called passive smoking-related lung cancer.

- Pregnant smokers have a higher chance of not reaching their full term in pregnancy.

- Children are more likely to smoke if they live with parents who both smoke, compared with children whose parents do not smoke.

- Children growing up in a household where smoking around them is normal are more likely to get pneumonia, bronchitis, asthma and ear infections.

Are my pets affected by smoking?

Pets are like humans in many ways, including their ability to catch diseases, be affected by chemicals in tobacco and get long-term and life-threatening conditions.

When people smoke in enclosed spaces, the smoke and the toxins within stay around in the air and on surfaces.

Most animals lick themselves clean so transfer of these harmful chemicals into their body is highly likely.

- Cats. Are more likely to suffer from feline lymphoma, (cancer), and get cat flu, aggravated feline asthma, heart problems, stomach upsets, skin allergies to the chemicals in cigarettes and other respiratory problems such as sneezing and coughing.

- Dogs. Are more likely to suffer from respiratory problems such as coughing, sneezing and also lung, nasal or sinus cancer, (especially long-nosed dogs). They can also suffer from repeated stomach upsets and heart problems.

- Indoor birds, (especially budgies). Are also much more likely to develop respiratory problems including pneumonia and other chest infections as they cannot filter their lungs.

'Pets are like humans in many ways, including their ability to catch diseases, be affected by chemicals in tobacco and get long-term and life-threatening conditions.'

If your pets are on medications for diabetes, epilepsy, respiratory, heart and other problems, then they can also have the same problems that humans have with tobacco smoke. Animal medications are often the same as human ones and can be sent out of the body quicker if tobacco smoke is present.

Nicotine is a stimulant and pets in homes of particularly heavy smokers have also gone through an equivalent of nicotine withdrawal. After a period of time, the pets, like their owners, usually seem to be more relaxed.

What makes smoking so harmful?

What the tobacco companies don't want you to know:

'Tobacco smoke contains over 4,000 different substances.'

If you met Sir Walter Raleigh now and he said, 'I've got this great new fun stick that contains road-covering chemicals, varnish, strong detergents, bits of metal, stuff you pickle body parts in and, oh yes, waste products of mammals. You can be hooked in seconds and after a lifetime of smoking you can make yourself poor, ill, dead or disabled.' What would your reply be? Yet this is exactly what smoking entails.

Tobacco smoke contains over 4,000 different substances. They are added for many reason reasons – from improving the taste and smell, to making the product grow. Some are absorbed in the planting and growing stages or, in the case of substances like ammonia, are added to make you absorb nicotine quicker and get more hooked even in the low nicotine brands.

The chemicals that are found in cigarettes:

- Acetone – Nail varnish remover.
- Ammonia – A heavy duty disinfectant.
- Arsenic – A poison used in insecticides.
- Benzene – A solvent found in many chemicals and petrol fuel.
- Butane – Lighter fuel.
- Cadnium – A poisonous metal found in batteries.

- Carbon monoxide – This sticks to red blood cells, reducing the ability to carry oxygen around the body. It changes the shape (and oxygen-carrying capabilities) of the red blood cells and makes them sticky, leading to a greater chance of blocked arteries.

- Cresol – Found in disinfectants, photographic processing compounds and fence paint.

- Formaldehyde – Found in hospitals and laboratories for preserving bodies.

- Hydrogen cyanide – A deadly poison.

- Lead – A harmful substance found in old pipes and roof tiles.

- Magnesium – An element and a compound found in alloy car wheels.

- Nicotine – The addictive component, not known to be cancer-causing but also used as an insecticide.

- Polonium 210 – A radioactive substance that reportedly killed a Russian in London a few years ago.

- Radon – Another radioactive substance.

- Shellac – A sweet-smelling substance found in varnish.

- Sulphuric acid – A strong cleaning acid.

- Tar – Like the road covering. This narrows the lung airways and causes coughing and cancer.

- Urea – A human, (or animal), waste product.

'It is really easy to stop smoking. It is staying stopped that's the hard part.'

But we know all that. The health issues have been well publicised and in truth rarely motivate on their own. That's why it is important to look for other reasons that motivate you as well as health. Hopefully when you stop, your health will sort itself out in time.

It is really easy to stop smoking. It is staying stopped that's the hard part.

We can all stop something for a minute, an hour, a day, but real change only comes when behaviour and thinking is also changed.

I have seen many people battle with the health issues but still miss cigarettes. Wouldn't it be better to also look at reasons closer to home?

Reasons, excuses and legends

The smoker's top 10

The way to challenge these thoughts will be shown in more detail in Chapter 3.

Many smokers use the following excuses to justify why, what, how and when they smoke, which ones in the list can you relate to?

'It helps me to concentrate.'

'It's my only vice.'

'It relieves stress.'

'It makes me look older.'

'It helps me join in.' (Socialise).

'It keeps my weight down.'

'I enjoy it.'

'It relieves boredom.'

'Low-tar cigarettes are healthier.'

'Cigars do not have the same problems as cigarettes.'

If you have different ones, don't forget to add them to your list.

So, if those were the excuses to keep you smoking, what are the reasons to stop?

Why smokers want to stop

'For health.'

'To save money.'

'For my family and friends.'

'My teeth are stained.'

'I've started feeling unhealthy generally.'

'I'm fed up of my hair, clothes and home smelling of tobacco smoke.'

'I hate being treated like a second class citizen and having to go out in the rain on my breaks.'

'I want to take control back, as I hate a bunch of leaves in a bit of paper/pipe controlling me.'

'As a secret smoker, I find I have to lie to my loved ones and I don't like the deceit.'

Have you got reasons to add to this list?

Summing Up

- Smoking tobacco has been cited as the hardest addiction to overcome, (even by ex-heroin addicts).

- If it is your choice to stop then you are making a good start, but if other people are telling you to stop, then that is harder.

- There are many reasons why people smoke and also why they want to stop, with many triggers that cause you to slip up along the way.

- It is up to you to find your own reasons to stop, to choose medications that will help and work out how you will change your thinking and routines to those of a non-smoker.

- It is your addiction and it is you that has to change that.

- It is not about giving up smoking but more about choosing not to pick one up again.

- You are much more likely to stay stopped if you believe that tobacco is no longer useful and you love life without it.

'It is your addiction and it is you that has to change that.'

Chapter Two

Medications and Reducing Physical Withdrawal Symptoms

To understand why medications help, it is worth looking at the subject of nicotine withdrawal and what happens when people stop smoking.

Smokers often expect the medications to do more than they can. The medicines can't change the way you think about cigarettes or how you run your day-to-day life.

In our modern society, we forget this sometimes and often believe there is a pill for everything. When planning to stop smoking you need to make sure you look after yourself well so that your body can recover quickly. Below are some suggested remedies to common problems so that your experience of stopping smoking is as comfortable as possible.

'The medicines can't change the way you think about cigarettes or how you run your day-to-day life.'

What withdrawal and recovery symptoms should I expect?

▪ Constipation. Nicotine is a stimulant and has a laxative effect. A non-medical remedy for constipation is a good diet with plenty of exercise and to drink lots of fluids.

▪ Coughing or sore throat. Your lungs are rejecting the tar and debris that has built up over the years.

- Mouth ulcers and acne type spots. These are due to some of the chemicals in cigarettes which act as disinfectants and kill minor bacteria. When people stop smoking, these chemicals are absent and until immunity is strengthened, people who are stopping smoking are more likely to get minor infections in the upper respiratory tract and oral cavity and face.

- Physical cravings. They usually last a few minutes.

- Difficulty concentrating. This is caused by the brain adjusting to higher levels of oxygen due to less carbon monoxide and the absence of nicotine.

- Disturbed sleep or insomnia. This is completely normal as your body and brain adjust to being a non-smoker.

- Emotional or suffering from mood swings. Feeling tearful or really irritable can be for many reasons, including a process of change similar to grief. Tobacco smoke can also affect natural hormones and as such there may also be a slight imbalance as the body adjusts.

- Headaches, dizziness or tingling. This happens as the blood vessels all over your body are opening up.

- Increased appetite. A repairing body needs energy.

- Tiredness. This is normal in the early days of stopping smoking.

How long will withdrawal symptoms last?

- Constipation – 4 to 6 weeks.

- Coughing or sore throat – 4 to 6 weeks, (when the cilia grows back).

- Mouth ulcers and acne type spots – 2 to 4 weeks.

- Physical cravings – 2 to 10 weeks depending on medication usage.

- Difficulty concentrating – 1 week.

- Disturbed sleep or insomnia – 1 to 2 weeks.

- Being emotional or suffering from mood swings – 2 to 4 weeks.

- Headaches, dizziness or tingling – 1 to 2 weeks.

* Increased appetite – 10 weeks.

* Tiredness – 2 to 12 weeks.

These can be different for each person as we are all individuals and respond differently to certain situations.

If you look after yourself well during this time and have a few things to look forward to like meals out, cinema trips and other fun things planned, then your mood will pick up quickly and you will feel much better quickly.

In some people these symptoms can persist and are not always associated with just physical withdrawal. If they do, it is a good idea to talk it over with your GP in the first instance.

Will medicines help?

The main reason for all the Stop Smoking medications is to replace nicotine, or a similar substance, and control or reduce cravings and withdrawal symptoms while the patient continues to stop smoking. Some medications also block the effect tobacco has on your brain so the benefits of smoking are less.

Many people hope that the medicines available to help them stop smoking will be all that they need. Unfortunately, all the medications can do is give you time to change the way you think about cigarettes, how you experience your routines comfortably without cigarettes whilst strengthening your resolve to stay stopped.

Stop Smoking medications are available on the NHS and are divided into 2 groups:

* Nicotine replacement – patches, gum, lozenges, sublingual tablets, mouth spray, nasal spray and inhalator.

* Systemic treatments (tablets) – buproprion, (Zyban), and varenicline, (Champix).

'Many people hope that the medicines available to help them stop smoking will be all that they need. Unfortunately all the medications can do is give you time to change the way you think about cigarettes, how you experience your routines comfortably without cigarettes whilst strengthening your resolve to stay stopped.'

What if I am on other medications?

Smoking can also interfere with and reduce or increase the effects of some medications such as thyroxin, antidepressants, some psychiatric medications, asthma drugs, some heart and diabetes drugs, drugs used for respiratory problems and some painkillers.

You should discuss the possible effects with your GP before stopping smoking if you have any concerns at the beginning or at any time in the first few months of stopping.

Want to save some money?

If you do not pay prescription charges then going to a Stop Smoking service is a cost-effective option, as nicotine replacement can be expensive when bought over the counter.

If you pay prescription charges, the other Stop Smoking medications, even when bought at the usual prescription charge, can be expensive as they are usually prescribed every 2 weeks, (you will therefore need to budget for 6 prescriptions).

For those that have to pay and who have more than four prescriptions over 3 months, you can save money with the NHS pre-paid prescription certificate. You only pay the price of about four prescriptions for the certificate and then any other medications you are prescribed will be free, (even if they are not the Stopping Smoking medications but things such as asthma inhalers and painkillers). Call 0845 850 0030 for information to order by phone, access via the Internet on https://www.ppa.org.uk/ppa/ppcdd/patient.do.

You can also pick up an application form FP95 from your doctor's surgery or pharmacy. If you think you may be entitled to free prescriptions you can find out by going to http://www.nhsbsa.nhs.uk/HealthCosts/2131.aspx or calling 0845 609 9299.

'For those that have to pay prescription charges and who have more than four prescriptions over 3 months you can save money with the NHS pre-paid prescription certificate.'

Nicotine replacement therapy (NRT)

What does NRT do?

Nicotine replacement therapy replaces nicotine in a controlled way and reduces cravings and withdrawal symptoms while the patient remains smoke-free.

Nicotine patch

Patches are discreet and convenient once you have them on, allowing you to forget they are there and carry on with your day. They release a steady amount of nicotine into the skin throughout the day, and help to relieve some of the physical cravings for nicotine.

Depending on your needs, you can choose clear or skin colour versions.

How do I use nicotine patches?

- Patches can last either 16 hours, (take off an hour before bedtime), or 24 hours depending on your nicotine needs. Ask your GP, pharmacist, nurse or advisor to help you choose the right patch for you.

- They come in three stages, (steps 1 to 3). The step you start with and the amount of time you stay on each stage varies depending on the particular patch and the amount that you smoke in a day.

- It is best to change the site you put them on each day as this reduces the risk of irritation and allows the previous day's site time to recover.

- You should put the patch on a clean, dry and hairless area of skin. The most popular sites to apply the patches are on the upper arm, lower abdomen or thigh.

- Avoid broken areas of skin or tattoos (as nicotine can irritate them and cause soreness).

- If you have skin conditions or known allergies to patches or plasters you may get the same with the patches.

- They can now be used alongside other nicotine preparations.

Nicotine gum

Chewing nicotine gum releases nicotine through the lining of the mouth. They are available in 2mg and 4mg strengths and should be used when you feel cravings starting and also at regular intervals to prevent cravings becoming stronger.

Nicotine gum is particularly useful for those who generally enjoy chewing gum.

How do I use nicotine gum?

- It is important to use the gum regularly making sure you have enough pieces of gum in the day to avoid experiencing strong withdrawal symptoms and prevent going back to smoking. Usually 10 to 15 pieces a day.

- You normally use the 'chew and park' technique. You chew the gum until the taste gets strong and then park the gum at the side of your mouth until the taste gets less. You repeat this until you feel you have had enough. Usually this lasts around 30 minutes.

- 2mg nicotine gum is most effective for smokers of 20 cigarettes a day or less. The 4mg nicotine gum is most effective for smokers of more than 20 cigarettes a day or who have their first cigarette within 30 minutes of waking.

- Liquorice flavour is not suitable if you are pregnant as it can cause severe cramps.

Nicotine inhalator

The inhalator is small tube about the size of a cigarette with a cartridge containing nicotine within the tube.

Nicotine is absorbed through the lining of the mouth, not the lungs, and works best at room temperature.

It is a very popular medication and is often used as well as patches because it gives you something to do with your hands.

How do I use the nicotine inhalator?

- At the start, you may need to use 6-12 cartridges a day.

- Each cartridge can be used 2-3 times, although the number, frequency and duration of inhalations will vary depending on how you feel you need to use it.

- This is not the best product for people with asthma, and those with lung problems such as COPD often find it hard to use properly.

Nicotine sublingual tablet

The nicotine 2mg sublingual tablet is placed under the tongue and slowly disintegrates within 30 minutes providing a discreet alternative for those either not able or not wishing to use the other forms of nicotine.

How do I use the nicotine sublingual tablet?

It is suitable for both light and heavy smokers and you would normally take one to two tablets an hour. Up to 16 tablets can usually be taken daily but do not exceed 40.

Nicotine lozenge

The nicotine lozenge comes in strengths of 1, 2 or 4mg and they cater for the whole range of light and heavy smokers. They are most suitable for those who prefer the action of sucking and those who are unable or do not wish to have the other preparations that are available.

How do I use the nicotine lozenge?

- Suck the lozenge until it dissolves completely, using a similar 'park and rest' technique as nicotine gum.

- Do not chew or swallow the lozenges as this may reduce their effect.

- Use enough lozenges to improve the chance of success. Up to 15 a day.

- These lozenges contain sodium, (salt), so if you have high blood pressure or have been told to have a low sodium diet then the lozenges are not the best medication for you

Nicotine mini lozenges

This is a new medication and is a small tablet that rapidly dissolves in the mouth. It is available in strengths of 1.5mg and 2mg lozenges for the lighter smoker and 4mg lozenges for the heavier smoker.

How do I use the mini lozenges?

- Use up to 15 lozenges a day.
- It is free of salt so can be used as an alternative to the other nicotine lozenges.
- Being a small tablet, the mini lozenge provides a rapid but discreet alternative for those who are unable or do not wish to have the other preparations that are available.

Nicotine mouth spray

A nicotine solution is sprayed into the mouth and is absorbed via the lining of the mouth. The spray starts to take effect within a few minutes, delivering nicotine faster than any other NRT.

It is, however, slower to deliver nicotine than a cigarette and is ideal for the highly dependent smokers who are either looking to stop completely or cut down.

How do I use the nicotine mouth spray?

- The recommended initial dose is 1 to 2 doses per hour.
- A dose is equal to one spray in each side of the mouth.
- Maximum dose is 64 sprays a day, (4 sprays per hour).

- Can cause local irritant side effects such as a sore throat, a burning sensation, hiccups, and nausea. These symptoms are usually mild and well tolerated. Dizziness has also been reported.

Nicotine nasal spray

Nicotine solution is sprayed into the nostrils and is absorbed via the lining of the nose. This is fast-acting nicotine and takes effect in around 10 minutes.

How do I use the nicotine nasal spray?

- Recommended initial dosage is 1 to 2 doses per hour.
- One dose is equal to one spray in each nostril.
- Can cause local irritation to the nose or throat, a runny nose and sneezing. These generally lessen with regular use.

Can I use two nicotine treatments at once?

Better results can be increased when you use two or more NRT products together. For example, if you use nicotine gum and a nicotine patch at the same time you increase your chance of staying stopped compared with a single treatment.

'Better results can be increased when you use two or more NRT products together.'

What do I need to know about nicotine replacement therapy?

- Apart from the patches, most of the oral nicotine preparation doses are reduced at three months.
- Most preparations, except for the patch and the nasal spray, are absorbed through the lining of the mouth so it is best to not have acidic drinks such as orange juice for 15 minutes before using the oral nicotine and for 15 minutes after.
- Nicotine replacement therapy is available at most supermarkets and chemists or can be obtained on prescription from your GP or NHS Stop Smoking services (where with support and guidance you can quadruple your chances of success).

Generally, what side effects can I expect from nicotine replacement therapy?

- Indigestion.

- Heartburn.

- Skin irritation, (mainly when using patches and nasal spray).

- Mouth ulcers. Mainly from the oral therapies but also as a result of stopping smoking.

- Sleep disturbance. Nightmares and vivid dreams mainly happen with the 24-hour patches.

Are there any new medications coming out?

Nicotine pouches are thought to be faster acting than the nicotine gum and are currently going through clinical trials. The plan is to launch them in the United Kingdom as a 4mg pouch and they may be faster in action than nicotine gum.

They work in a similar way to the lozenges as you place the nicotine pouch against your gums and they gradually dissolve. The side effects are expected to be much the same as for gum and include mouth irritation, nausea, and aggravation of mouth ulcers.

In 2012, a vaccine may be available that removes nicotine before it crosses into the brain making it take away the reward aspect associated with nicotine. This is currently under the final stages of trial and there is not much information available as yet.

Non-nicotine Stop Smoking medications

Bupropion (Zyban)

- Bupropion was being used as an antidepressant, when it was found to have properties that gave people less desire to smoke.

- Bupropion gradually increases to full dose on the seventh day of taking it.

- You still smoke for the first week and pick a day in the second week to stop smoking as the effect of bupropion, is gradual. The course usually lasts for 10 weeks and is prescribed by your GP. You are usually expected to attend a programme that includes behavioural support, (like the NHS Stop Smoking service), to obtain this medication.

Is bupropion suitable for everyone?

- People under 18, those who are pregnant and those who are still breastfeeding are not able to use this medication.

- Doctors are also cautious about prescribing bupropion if you have a history of alcohol abuse, past head injury, or a history of brain damage. They are also cautious if you have high blood pressure, take oral diabetic medicines or insulin, using stimulants, weight loss medications or antidepressants.

- It is also worth noting that you should not take bupropion if you are taking some natural herbal therapies such as St John's wort.

What side effects can I expect with bupropion (Zyban)?

Side effects such as seizures, headaches, dizziness, problems with sleeping, drowsiness or skin problems have all been reported. Having said all that, bupropion has been around for a long time and has proven to be a successful aid to stopping smoking.

What is varenicline (Champix)?

Varenicline (Champix) is a medication that reduces withdrawal symptoms and helps to take the pleasure out of smoking.

It does this by blocking the nicotine receptors so the nicotine from a cigarette has nowhere to go. The smoker finds the cigarette tastes unpleasant. They may also feel quite nauseous and throw the cigarette away.

'It is also worth noting that you should not take bupropion if you are taking some natural herbal therapies such as St John's wort.'

To prevent nausea, it is recommended that you take varenicline immediately after eating and with at least a good sized glass of water to wash it down.

To avoid difficulty sleeping, varenicline should not be taken late at night.

You usually smoke during the first week or two of taking the medication. Your quit day is set with your Stop Smoking advisor within the first two weeks of starting varenicline. The national prescribing licence insists that you access this medication through your local Stop Smoking service.

The trial data and experience show varenicline seems to show a higher than average success rate and makes this medication a popular choice.

It is not, however, a magic pill and behavioural change is still needed to ensure long-term success.

'To prevent nausea, it is recommended that you take varenicline immediately after eating and with at least a good sized glass of water to wash it down.'

Is varenicline (Champix) suitable for everyone?

- People under 18, those who are pregnant and those who are still breastfeeding are not able to use this medication.

- Doctors are also cautious about prescribing varenicline, for patients who are currently being treated for severe depression, have a history of some mental health problems or a history of suicidal behaviour.

What side effects can I expect with varenicline?

Side effects such as nausea, sleep disturbance, flatulence, trapped wind, constipation, cluster headaches have all been reported. There have also been suggestions that varenicline use is linked with mood changes, irritability, worsening depression and suicidal thoughts.

These reports have not been proven and anyone with concerns should have a chat with their doctor before deciding for or against using varenicline.

Many of these side effects are a normal response to stopping smoking, (the only licensed use for varenicline).

Getting extra support from the medicine manufacturers

Most of the makers of Stop Smoking medicines have extra support services, in the form of a website, support line, online forum or subscription-based, any extra help is welcome if you are struggling.

These services also give you valuable information and tips on how to make things a bit better for you in the first few weeks. They are normally free.

The NRT Manufacturers have the following support packages:

Active Stop Programme

Nicorette (McNeil Healthcare (UK) Limited): http://www.nicorette.co.uk/active-stop

The programme gives support via mobile phone, a daily email, the Internet and with an iPhone app.

Quitmasters

NiQuitin CQ, (GSK), provide their online interactive programme called 'Quitmasters' which helps you to track, target and address your moments of temptation and gives you a complete 'tailored toolkit of support, motivation and advice': http://niquitin.co.uk/quit-smoking-plan/quitmasters (last accessed 27 June 2011).

LifeRewards Scheme

For those who have been prescribed Champix there is the LifeRewards programme, (which is an interactive website built around daily articles and activities): https://www.myliferewards.co.uk/PAGES/PxWelcome.aspx (last accessed on 27 June 2011).

If you do not have access to the Internet, you can ring 0800 345 7905 for a hard copy version of the Life Rewards Programme You do need to have your medication package handy when subscribing online as they will want to know the batch number.

Summing Up

- The main reason for the Stop Smoking medications is to replace nicotine or a similar substance by controlling or reducing cravings and withdrawal symptoms.

- Some medications also block the effect tobacco has on your brain so the benefits of smoking are less.

- There are good points and bad points to all the medications, in the end it comes down to personal choice or preference.

- There is no such thing as a magic pill, but the better chances you have of controlling your physical symptoms, then the more able you are to change your thinking about cigarettes and changing your routines for the better.

- The medicines cannot change the way you think about cigarettes or how you run your day-to-day life, the purpose of the medication is to give you time to adjust.

'The medicines cannot change the way you think about cigarettes or how you run your day-to-day life, the purpose of the medication is to give you time to adjust.'

Chapter Three

Planning Your Stop Smoking Day

When do I plan my stop smoking day?

Having decided on medications that may help you with withdrawal symptoms, you now need to decide what to do about the other triggers (the thoughts you have about where you see smoking fitting into your life), and the daily rituals and routines that remind you of cigarettes.

You now need to work out how you will make cigarettes less useful in your mind and your life better without them.

When you are changing routines, try to make them as much fun as possible. An improved routine is far more likely to stay.

This process starts with thinking about some of the health benefits, followed by reviewing your thoughts about smoking, and looking at which situations will be hardest for you, in the interactive part of this chapter.

How fast do you see health benefits when you stop smoking?

- After 20 minutes – Blood pressure and heart rate start returning to normal levels.
- After 8 hours – Nicotine and carbon monoxide levels are halved and oxygen returns to normal levels.

'When you are changing routines, try to make them as much fun as possible. An improved routine is far more likely to stay.'

- After 24-48 hours – Carbon monoxide and nicotine have gone from the body. The lungs clear out mucus and debris and your sense of taste and smell begin to improve.
- After 72 hours – Breathing becomes easier and energy levels start to rise.
- 2-12 weeks – Circulation continues to improve.
- 3-9 months – Respiratory problems (such as coughing, wheezing and asthma) improve as the lung functions improve.
- 5 years + – The risk of heart attack falls to half that of a smoker.
- 10 years + – The risk of lung cancer drops to half that of a smoker and the risk of heart attack becomes the same as a 'never-smoker'.

Do cigarettes really help?

Think back to the work from the previous chapters. Are there any thoughts that keep you smoking and have made you go back to smoking in the past?

Any of these sound familiar?

- 'It helps me concentrate.' Nicotine is a stimulant but in reality the effect is short-lived. The addictive nature of smoking causes the inability to concentrate, distracting the mind with cravings in the first place until the body's craving for nicotine is fulfilled. Carbon monoxide reduces concentration further, due to the lower oxygen levels to the brain.
- 'It's my only vice.' Do you really need to have any vices? Have you reached the state of mind that you do not enjoy smoking due to the control it has over you? How do you feel having to stand in the cold? What about that cough in the morning? Is this vice really worth it?
- 'It relieves stress.' But does it really? Smoking is a stimulant which increases the amount of adrenaline in the body. Nicotine increases the anxious state. Most ex-smokers become calmer (in time).
- 'It makes me look older.' Yes it does, it dries out the skin and increases wrinkles. It also makes hair prematurely grey!

- 'It helps me join in (socialise).' This has become harder as new smoke-free legislation takes hold and reduces meeting places where you can smoke. If there is nothing in the cigarette to change your personality, will becoming a non-smoker really reduce your ability to socialise?

- 'It keeps my weight down.' There are better ways of doing this. Most studies show that the difference in weight is usually just a few pounds, (kilograms). More weight can be put on if food is used as a substitute to cigarettes. Granted, nicotine does stimulate metabolism but so does exercise and other lifestyle changes which become more enjoyable when smoking ceases and energy increases.

- 'I enjoy it.' Are you sure? Exactly what is it that you enjoy? Most smokers freely state that they wish to give up smoking and many try several times before succeeding. If it was really enjoyable then why are there so many reasons you want to stop?

- 'It relieves boredom.' How does the cigarette achieve this? Do you really need something to do with your hands and does it have to be a cigarette? What else could you do that is fun instead? Any hobbies you would like to take up or start again?

- 'My aunt/uncle died at 98 years old, drank 2 bottles of whisky a night and smoked 40 a day and it did them no harm.' Yes, there are stories like that but what happens if it does cause you harm? What happens if they were lucky but you did not inherit the luck? No one has to give up smoking, it is your choice, but once again I would recommend looking at all your other reasons and asking yourself, is it worth the risk?

- 'My friend gave up and immediately contracted cancer or heart disease, so if I give up will it make me feel worse?' Often smoking can mask symptoms of other disorders. When you give up smoking, you have the help and regular access to health professionals who often notice things you would not. Being already under their care, you would then be referred for tests quicker and existing disorders could then be uncovered. In short, stopping smoking cannot bring on cancer and often stopping smoking reduces risks and helps treatments for many disorders to work better. Life happens whilst the process of quitting goes on and sadly, for some, their health may already be bad. It may also be why they had the instinct or advice to stop in the first place.

- 'Low-tar, low-nicotine cigarettes are healthier, so surely I can use these and just cut down.' There is still the issue of all the other harmful chemicals in cigarettes including cancer-causing tar. There are studies that suggest many low-tar cigarette smokers also puff on the cigarettes harder to get the nicotine out, (this is called 'compensation'). Tobacco companies tried to contest their right to market low-tar and low-nicotine cigarettes ('Lights') as a healthier option, but, even they did not have evidence to back up the claim. The sale of so-called 'light' cigarettes has largely been stamped out now as studies showed little benefit and some even suggested that low yield cigarettes may even increase the chance of cancer. It is now well recognised that no cigarette is a safe cigarette. Cutting down tends to work for a short while but soon creeps up again. The best way to stop smoking is to stop completely.

- 'Pipe smoking is healthier.' Pipe smokers have the same risk of getting lung cancer and other illnesses as cigarette smokers. The degree of risk with any tobacco increases with the amount smoked.

- 'Cigars do not have the same problems as cigarettes.' Cigar smoke creates up to 30 times more carbon monoxide, (and up to 25 times more environmental tobacco smoke than cigarettes). This means there is less oxygen being delivered throughout your body. Cigar smokers suffer higher rates of cancers of the mouth, tongue, throat and voice box than cigarette smokers. Cigar additives are not regulated and are not required to be reported to the government or to the public.

Can you think of anymore 'excuses'?

How using a smoker's diary starts the process of change

Now to put it all together. This section is designed so that you can find out the issues relating to you and customise your approach to your needs.

The smoker's diary is a good place to start. Consider what time you smoke, what you are doing as well as smoking and why you had the cigarette.

Now consider what you will change about that routine when you are a non-smoker.

Time	Monday	Tuesday	Wednesday	Thursday	Friday
7am					
8am					
9am					
10am					
11am					
12noon					
1pm					
2pm					
3pm					
4pm					
5pm					
6pm					
7pm					
8pm					
9pm					
10pm					
11pm					
12pm					
1am					
2am					
3am					
4am					
5am					
6am					

'Consider what time you smoke, what you are doing as well as smoking and why you had the cigarette. Now consider what you will change about that routine when you are a non-smoker.'

What can knock my confidence? Testing the thinking

As well as addictive thinking, for some people there are the negative thoughts which sap confidence when making a lifestyle change.

The table below is there to help you identify some of these thoughts and then reframe them into positives rather than negatives.

Negative thought pattern	Examples	Put into context	Your positive thought
All or nothing thinking	'If I don't give smoking up now, I never will'	No pressure then. Many say this and go on to succeed, how do you know what the future holds? Where is the evidence? Is it really a pleasure?	
Generalisation	'It's just who I am' 'No one really stops, they all go back eventually'	Are you sure? Where is the evidence that everyone goes back to smoking?	
Concentrating on the negative	'I will never succeed' 'I'm weak-willed' 'What's the point in trying, it won't work'	Where is the evidence? To be a smoker it takes strong will, (who likes to stand out smoking in a gale), so is this true?	
Putting the problem to the extreme	'I'm far too stressed all the time to stop smoking' 'It will all end badly'	If I try this would I be more or less stressed in reality? Where is the evidence?	
Bargaining	'I know I am not addicted to nicotine so I can give up any time.' 'I need cigarettes to keep me calm', 'If I put on weight, I will go back to smoking.'	Is it fact? Is it really? What is the realistic effect of continuing as I am? What would be the effect of change?	

Can I do it myself now?

Thought diary			
Thought	Negative thought pattern	Put into context	Your positive thought

Summarising the plan

How many cigarettes do I smoke a day? ....

How much does it cost me?

▦ £ per day ....

▦ £ per week..

▦ £ per month..

▦ £ per year ....

What could I do with this money instead?

....

....

What were my 5 main reasons for smoking?

▦ ....

▦ ....

▦ ....

▦ ....

▦ ....

How will I overcome these?

....

....

What are my 5 main reasons for stopping smoking?

▦ ....

▦ ....

▦ ....

▦ ....

▦ ....

How will I feel when I am smoke-free? How did I feel last time I was smoke-free?

....

....

What else do I need to change?

....

....

How will I make things fun?

....

....

What routines will I change?

....

....

What day will be my 'stop' day? (Pick a day when you are most likely to succeed rather than one where you may really struggle.)

....

....

What treats or goals can I plan to spur me on?

- On day 1 I will...
- On day 3 I will...
- At the end of my first week I will...
- At the end of my first month I will...

'Pick a day when you are most likely to succeed rather than one where you may really struggle.'

Summing up

- All the information has been gathered together, you know why you want to stop, which day you will stop and how to avoid your main triggers.

- You have looked at your routines and decided what you will do instead and have planned some fun things to look forward to during your first few weeks to spur you along a bit.

- To imagine yourself as a non-smoker is hard for many and my advice is to take each day as it comes.

- You will need the support from loved ones and you need to make sure you also have time for yourself to adjust to your new routines and life without cigarettes.

- Be nice to yourself and have some fun.

- Do something special on your first day, and at other milestones, because if you have something to look forward to, the wobbly moments pass a bit easier.

Chapter Four

The First Few Days and Weeks

If your life is better as a non-smoker and cigarettes seem to be useless, then the likelihood of going back to smoking will become quite small.

Let's see what you can expect in the first few weeks.

Start looking for the benefits from day one

Are you seeing any of these benefits yet?

- After 20 minutes – Blood pressure and heart rate starts returning to normal levels.

- After 8 hours – Nicotine and carbon monoxide levels are halved and oxygen returns to normal levels.

- After 24-48 hours – Carbon monoxide and nicotine has gone from the body. The lungs clear out mucus and debris and a sense of taste and smell begins to improve.

- After 72 hours – Breathing becomes easier and energy levels start to rise.

- 2-12 weeks – Circulation continues to improve.

- 3-9 months – Respiratory problems, (such as coughing, wheezing, asthma) improve as the lung functions improve.

- 5 years + – The risk of heart attack falls to half that of a smoker.

'If your life is better as a non-smoker and cigarettes seem to be useless, then the likelihood of going back to smoking will become quite small.'

- 10 years + – The risk of lung cancer drops to half that of a smoker and the risk of heart attack becomes the same as a 'never-smoker'.

Not everyone's journey is the same

You may already be seeing some of the early health benefits listed previously.

If you are that is great but if not, sometimes these can take longer.

- Some people feel worse before they feel better. This is especially so for people with conditions such as asthma or COPD.
- People with conditions involving blood flow, the nervous system, joints and bones can experience a slight increase in pain at first but this soon settles after a few weeks.
- Other people have a massive change very quickly, for these, giving up smoking shows just how much smoking was harming them on a daily basis.
- Minor coughs in the morning can disappear very quickly and even snoring for some. (Usually a great relief to their partners!)

What other benefits will I see?

The health benefits keep the medical professionals happy but what about the ones that hit the heart of the matter for you.

Are you seeing any of these yet?

- Are your children smiling yet because they have, or will have, a fitter parent?
- Are you feeling that you have taken back control?
- Do you have more money for treats?
- Have you had extra visits to the cinema, restaurant, theme parks, book shop, gym?
- Have you had any 'retail therapy' yet?
- Have you started your favourite hobby yet?
- Have you had any other life improvements not listed here?

What are the recovery symptoms?

As well as physical withdrawal from nicotine, your body is already experiencing changes, (recovery symptoms). It needs time to adjust and to remove toxins from the body.

There are many ways to help with these symptoms and some are covered below.

If the problems persist and you are concerned, ask your GP, nurse or pharmacist for advice.

How can I manage the recovery symptoms?

- Constipation. Nicotine is a stimulant and has a laxative effect. A well-balanced diet including five pieces of either fruit or vegetables can help, along with drinking lots of fluids. Exercise helps keep everything moving. If the problem continues then speak to your pharmacist, GP or nurse and they may be able to recommend medications to help until your body settles. Symptoms usually ease in a few weeks.

- Coughing or sore throat. Your lungs are rejecting the tar and debris that has built up over the years. Good news, the small hairs, (cilia), that help force debris up and out of the respiratory tract are starting to grow back and they have their work cut out cleaning out the lungs. The lungs can also feel strange as they feel more elastic and it is common to feel a bit breathless. Normal sore throat remedies help to relieve symptoms and some herbal remedies can help.

- Cravings. These generally only last a few minutes. Try taking several deep breaths, taking sips of water and doing things you enjoy to distract yourself. Ask yourself whether these are true cravings or just a reminder that you used to smoke at that time? Many changes in routines feel strange to start with. You will soon get used to being a non-smoker. Take heart, it does get easier in time.

- Difficulty concentrating. The brain is adjusting to higher levels of oxygen, less carbon monoxide and the absence of nicotine. The body is fighting hard to repair the damage smoking has done and get the body right again,

'As well as physical withdrawal from nicotine, your body is already experiencing changes, (recovery symptoms). It needs time to adjust and to remove toxins from the body.'

this can also sap the energy. It is a period of change and sometimes change can be tiring. Make sure you take care of yourself and eat well to heal. You will soon be bursting with energy again (usually within a week).

> 'Endorphins are the natural happiness-inducing chemicals in the body which relieve stress, anger, anxiety and pain. Laughter and fun will produce a lot, (if not more), of the endorphins that smoking used to produce. Try to have as much fun as you can.'

- Disturbed sleep, dreams and insomnia. This is completely normal as your body and brain adjust to being a non-smoker. Sleep normally improves in a week or two. It is also common to dream that you have had a cigarette and feel devastated when you first wake up. Some medications can also disturb sleep, so make sure you take them as directed. Sometimes, as you get fitter and healthier, you need less sleep.

- Emotional or suffering from mood swings. Feeling tearful or really irritable can be common. Some people go through a grief process when they stop smoking. This will ease as time goes on. Tobacco smoke can affect natural chemicals such as hormones. These are sent out of the body quicker as a smoker and when you stop smoking, it takes time for the natural chemicals to settle to their normal levels. Remember it does get better in time, (usually two to four weeks).

- Headaches, dizziness or tingling. Blood vessels all over your body are opening up. So are the nerve endings. Headaches and dizziness could also be due to the increase in oxygen levels the brain is now receiving (often the body reacts the same when it has too much or little of the same chemicals). This will usually settle in a couple of weeks.

- Increased appetite. A repairing body needs energy. Fresh fruit, dried fruit and fruit juices are all great sources of natural energy and in reasonable amounts won't pile on the pounds. This can last up to ten weeks.

- Tiredness. This is normal in the early days of stopping smoking but can last anywhere up to 12 weeks so make sure you look after yourself well. You have much healing to do and the body needs to borrow some of your energy for a while.

To avoid most of these symptoms, make sure you look after yourself, even pamper yourself where you can.

Endorphins are the natural happiness-inducing chemicals in the body which relieve stress, anger, anxiety and pain. Laughter and fun will produce a lot, (if not more), of the endorphins that smoking used to produce.

Try to have as much fun as you can. Exercise that increases the heartbeat (aerobic) is another very good source of endorphins. Studies currently in progress, are showing great results in craving reduction in people stopping smoking whilst undergoing a programme of regular exercise.

Exercise is another good way to prevent another concern smokers have (weight gain) and get fit at the same time.

What else can I do to motivate me?

* Tea and coffee. Caffeine can be a physical trigger and if you can, it is best to reduce your intake. If you can't stand being without caffeine then why not change the routine a bit? You may find that by changing the experience, it reminds you that you are now making a different choice. Why not make sure you get your absolute favourite brand in and a new mug (a china one if you love tea as this apparently improves the taste and experience). You could decide to have your drink in a different room to where you used to drink and smoke. If a new routine is better then why go back to the old one?

* A favourite meal. A loved one may want to treat you on your first day, week, month, and this is one of the most popular ways they can help you.

* A spa weekend. Another popular idea usually taken on the first few days of stopping smoking. Relaxation and detox, what could be better?

* Girls' or lads' night out. Remember though that alcohol receptors are similar to nicotine receptors and they can trigger both physical and psychological cravings so make sure your friends know not to give you any cigarettes.

* A big holiday. Bought with all the money you saved.

* A new car. A new one or even a hefty valet to your old one so that you don't want to spoil it again by returning to smoking.

* Motorbike. Hard to smoke on one of these.

* A new activity. Such as music lessons, dance classes, salsa, 'dancercise' sessions or a gym membership helping to channel that irritability and enjoy a new interest.

This list is only limited by the imagination. Have I forgotten any?

How do I avoid the 'gremlin from within'?

Remember the old-fashioned cartoons, how when you made a decision, your conscience was shown as a little red being on one shoulder and a little white one on the other?

This is often how the mind decides things, it weighs up the risk versus the benefit, and sometimes also what we can get away with.

The same goes for addictive thinking, the 'gremlins from within'.

The vast majority of the population smoked through the 1950s, 1960s and even up to the 1970s. In the 1980s smoking started to decline. Until then, smoking was seen as cool in the movies, television programmes and adverts and within many social circles.

Even people who have never smoked have some opinion on how they think tobacco helps smokers.

I have even heard health care professionals tell patients to have a cigarette as they seem stressed.

Having dealt with all your common beliefs regarding tobacco in the previous chapters, you may find some new thoughts creeping in as the addictive part of your brain struggles to regain control again. This is normal. Your brain is just trying a last ditch attempt to tempt you back.

Remind yourself, why do you dislike cigarettes again?

Is grief part of the process?

Yes.

The grief is less as your desire to stop smoking increases and seeing the cigarettes as useful decreases.

The feeling of grief is usually worse in people who have been forced to stop smoking, but who feel they have lost their best friend but many people go through this stage.

What are the stages of grief?

- Denial – 'I can be a social smoker, I am not really addicted'.

- Depression – 'I feel down', 'There is something really missing'.

- Anger – 'How is it that some people just stop', 'What do the doctors know anyway, bet they smoke'.

- Bargaining – 'Just one can't do any harm surely?', 'I'll stop tomorrow'.

- Acceptance – 'I feel good, I knew that I would', 'I am better off without them', 'Cigarettes are rubbish, don't need them at all'.

These do not run in a cycle as many believe but can crop up throughout the day and in any order they like.

These feelings are normal and they will pass.

When you have trained up the little white gremlin on the shoulder a bit more, the little red gremlin won't stand a chance.

How do I banish the tough ones?

'Just one won't do any harm will it?'

('Bargaining' or a 'deal with the dark side'.) The reality is that one cigarette will trigger the nicotine receptors which will cause you to want more. One leads to another, and another. Ask any smoker who went back to smoking and it often started with 'just this one'. The close relative of this is 'I'll just buy a packet of ten as it won't do any harm' (denial). It also creates an open door to do it again if you 'get away with it' once.

'Well, I've cut down so I'm not doing that bad and I have smoked for 40 years'.

Perhaps, but, as above, one dose of tobacco wakes up the nicotine receptors and the internal nagging starts. Eventually you are right back to where you started. You may be smoking fewer cigarettes but you may be smoking them harder, taking in *more* nicotine and carbon monoxide than before. There are not many people who cut down and stay down.

'I'll just be a social smoker'.

There are very few people who can be 'just be a social smoker'. Often the smoking around the routine itself is the problem. It is worth reminding yourself why you dislike the cigarettes enough to stop them and whether it was the social occasion rather than the cigarette you enjoyed the most.

'If I get tetchy, my wife will force me to smoke again'.

What have you decided to do about how you handle stress? Have you decided to miss some regular breaks? (You need regular times during the day to allow your body and mind to rest, best to keep the break but not the cigarette). What about other ways of calming down, like walking away, taking five minutes out? Nicotine is a stimulant, (the opposite to a calming drug), could it always have been you that solved the problem? Also, your brain is very good at remembering you have not had a cigarette for a while, it could be that the addictive process is relieved 7 to 15 seconds after puffing on a cigarette as the nicotine gets to the brain and relieves that internal nagging. Think about that physical relief for a minute, how does it really feel, have you felt it before? Could this physical relief be similar to that feeling of relief when you let go of that heavy shopping bag when you get home, or stepping into a warm house after walking on a cold winter's day? For some, that is exactly how it is. Most people are calmer without cigarettes (in time).

'Buying ten isn't as bad as buying twenty is it?'

Yes, it will soon lead to buying twenties.

'It doesn't count as smoking as I never buy cigarettes but my friends do give them to me'.

It won't be long before you have to buy some and then you are back to square one.

Triggers to be aware of

Social occasions and alcohol

Alcohol is a physical trigger in itself as alcohol receptors in the brain are very similar to nicotine receptors and they can set off each other. This trigger, combined with strong associations, such as a drink in one hand and a cigarette the other whilst seeing your usual smoking friends, can make cravings very likely in this situation.

Suggestions to help with this include:

- Deciding to avoid social gatherings for a bit.

- Deciding that you won't hold friends' cigarettes for them as this can be too much temptation.

- Asking friends to help you by not offering you cigarettes, to remind you that you asked them and to stop you heading for the cigarette machine shop.

- Changing what you drink, as this reminds you of your choice to do things differently in a visual, taste and tactile way. It acts as a sort of red light saying 'this is different for a reason'.

Caffeine

This stimulates the nicotine receptors and is often associated with strong routines in the day. If you cannot do without your coffee or tea, try changing your favourite brand, changing where you have your drink, limiting the amount you have or even buying a new mug or cup to remind you of your choice to change.

After a meal

You may decide to get straight up and wash-up, (changing the routine), or have a glass of orange juice or a piece of fruit. You could try sitting in a different room to usual. However you do it, reviewing whether the cigarette

'Alcohol is a physical trigger in itself as alcohol receptors in the brain are very similar to nicotine receptors and they can set off each other.'

really played a part or whether there are better things you can do will help. Cravings only last a short time and are not life-threatening (even though sometimes they may feel that way).

The 'sin bin'

Could you still interact with your friends without following them out to the smoking area? If not, do you really need to smoke with them? Could you ask them to help you by not offering them to you?

The insecure smoking buddy

Sometimes there are friends out there that keep deliberately offering you cigarettes to 'test' you. If you get a really pushy smoking colleague that tries to get you back to smoking so they don't lose their smoking buddy, try taking one, breaking it in half and politely giving it back to them reaffirming that you no longer smoke, (they usually do not repeat the offer).

Down time for Mum, Dad or carer

Do you really need a cigarette to give you permission to take five minutes? The people we care about can be all-consuming sometimes (I know, I have been a single parent myself) and it is important to keep stress down and have 5 minutes. Some people find a simple task somewhere nearby can give them five minutes to themselves without being too far away. This task could be fairly mundane and require little thought (like putting shopping or washing away). Sometimes, doing a gentle task like watching a video with the children, distracting them with art and crafts can help. Setting down rules like parent's down time can be negotiated with the older children, (with the phrase 'do not disturb unless the house is falling down' proving to be a popular choice).

Cigarettes gave you five minutes away from the children to chill out and gather your thoughts, if you don't find an alternative you are likely to reach for the cigs.

Ask your non-smoking friends how they cope.

Parental life can be hard sometimes and the rest breaks are part of looking after your health. Look after yourself too because if you are ill, who will look after them?

Smoking while watching TV

How do you feel watching a programme with no adverts breaks? Do you wish the end of the programme would come so you can have a cigarette? Do you miss parts of the programme to have a cigarette?

How about a room makeover and making the house smoke-free?

On long car journeys

Initially, due to the stimulant effect of nicotine, you concentrate better for a few minutes but as oxygen levels decrease your brain starts nagging you for more nicotine, your concentration levels can deteriorate quicker than that of a non-smoker.

Your carbon monoxide levels increase as you become more tired and the cravings distract you.

If you have children in the car for up to two hours, carbon monoxide levels can be up to ten times more concentrated than if you smoked inside your house (even with the windows open).

The authorities in the UK are currently looking into banning smoking in cars where children are present and in some countries this is already the case due to the well-documented harm of environmental tobacco smoke.

Did you know that people have been charged with a driving offence because they smoked whilst driving?

It has been argued that you often don't have both hands on the wheel whilst smoking and driving (driving without full control). You may have your view temporarily blocked while lighting a cigarette when driving (driving without due care and attention).

People have also been charged for dropping their cigarette ends (littering).

These cases are rare but may be something worth thinking about.

So, does it really help you drive?

Driving around town and in traffic

Many smokers will state it calms them down, or relieves the boredom of town driving. When you completed your smoker's diary, you may find that this has become a hard routine to crack. There may be particular landmarks that remind you of cigarettes.

Could it be that you light up when you get in the car? When you exit the work car park, at the first set of lights on the way home to or from work?

You may decide to have mints or something else to replace the cigarettes at these times, or a nicotine inhalator.

Some people valet their car so that it looks and smells far too nice to smoke in, thus reducing the temptation even further.

Others take different routes to get out of their comfort zone for a while.

Walking the dog

You have done this every day for the dog's life and it now feels strange without the accompanying cigarette. You know every branch, lamp post and grassy patch and, like with driving, you have your light-up spots that constantly remind you that you used to smoke.

Time to change the routine?

Have you considered changing your route or the walk times for a while? How about walking a bit further and seeing the benefits of the new healthier you? How about going on even more walks? Many a dog has been worn out by these new extra walks, but both pet and owner have reaped the fitness rewards.

Summing Up

- There are many triggers, routines and thoughts at the disposal of the addictive part of your mind (the little red guy on your shoulder that says you still want cigarettes). By training the other side of the brain (the little white guy who will remind you that you want to be smoke-free) to argue against those thoughts, you will begin to find things get easier.

- In time that conscience-type conversation will change from you being very aware of those thoughts to them becoming a distant whisper, as both battle in your subconscious, (with only the occasional argument overheard).

- However you change your routines, try to make them better than the old ones. When the addictive thoughts come, question them, test the evidence and the logic of that belief. If cigarettes are not as useful as you thought and life is better without them, it is much easier to stay away from them.

Chapter Five

Stopping Smoking and Managing Weight

Is there more I can do to avoid gaining weight?

This is a common question posed by both men and women giving up smoking.

It often arises because, on previous attempts to stop smoking, they have gained too much weight.

I am not an authority on weight management so I will just be passing on a few simple tips that have either worked for my patients in the past or are pretty much mentioned in most other publications about smoking.

Have you noticed that smokers come in all shapes and sizes?

If the answer is yes, then it proves the belief that smoking helps to keep your weight down is unfounded, and there are better ways to control your weight.

If smoking was so good at keeping the weight down, is it not logical to assume that most smokers would be on average a bit lighter and that heavy smokers would be a lot lighter?

Any pharmacist, GP or nurse will give you excellent advice about maintaining a healthy diet, exercise and avoiding cigarettes.

'If smoking was so good at keeping the weight down, is it not logical to assume that most smokers would be on average a bit lighter and that heavy smokers would be a lot lighter?

Here are a few tips:

Where does blood sugar fit in?

A common reason people will snack to substitute cigarettes in the evening is often due to a lower blood glucose level, (blood sugar) than normal.

Tobacco smoke removes insulin from the body quicker and so less glucose is used up. When you stop smoking, more insulin remains so glucose is used up in the body and cravings for sweet foods are the body's attempt to compensate.

Having three meals a day containing healthy carbohydrate levels helps to maintain sugar levels.

And metabolism changes?

Nicotine is a stimulant and increases the metabolism. You can gain some weight due to changes in metabolism alone but this equates to only a few pounds or kilos. There have been some people who have gained up to a stone but this tends to be a lesser amount than people think.

This weight gain, with a normal balanced diet and exercise will come off within a year of stopping smoking and may be minimal when taking some Stop Smoking medications.

How does weight distribution figure?

It has been found that smokers are more likely to distribute weight (fat) around the vital organs, known as being 'apple-shaped'. It has been found that non-smokers are more likely to be the healthier 'pear shape'.

This distribution is important as it is now the measurement used together with the standard Body Mass Index (BMI) in the assessment of healthy weight and health risk. If you are 'apple-shaped', your major organs (such as heart and lungs) are restricted in movement by the fat pressing down on them. If you are 'apple-shaped' you are also more likely to have heart disease.

'It has been found that smokers are more likely to distribute weight, (fat) around the vital organs, known as being "apple-shaped". It has been found that non -mokers are more likely to be the healthier "pear shape".'

So, the weight management properties are not what you might expect. In short, smokers create a worse weight problem due to a more harmful weight spread and body shape.

Is taste a trigger?

When you stop smoking food often tastes better and so you need to be careful not to pander too much to the new (and in early stages very sensitive) taste buds. Your taste buds can lead you astray and before you know it you are trying all sorts of new flavours, not all of which are healthy and 'slenderising'.

Time?

Smokers may often have a cigarette instead of food (or with a smaller lunch). When you consider that a cigarette can take 5 to 10 minutes, and if you have travel time to the 'sin bin' (smokers' haunt) and a short lunch, it is often a choice of either cigarette or lunch. When stopping smoking, some people introduce extra foods (such as pudding) now they have time (and taste buds). This introduction of extra foods can quickly lead to weight gain.

If this is likely to happen to you, it is best to introduce low-calorie foods, such as fruits or yoghurts as an alternative to high-calorie puddings.

Any other tips on diet and exercise?

- Instead of extra food, try sips of water to satisfy some hunger pangs. Often this settles that little knot at the back of the throat.

- Try frozen fruit in the freezer (like frozen grapes) you can use these as a refreshing alternative to sweets.

- Look into what some weight management groups call 'free foods'.

- Ask yourself, is this just to substitute a cigarette? If yes, perhaps go for a walk, or do something else to distract yourself. The craving will soon pass.

- Take up a hobby that gives you something to do with your hands, or join a gym, dance class, cycling club or go swimming regularly. All of these will help with nicotine cravings, food pangs and also maintaining weight. They may be fun too.

- When driving to the shop, work or school, why not park on the far end of the car park and walk that extra few yards to add to your daily exercise routines. If it is a nice day and these places are not too far, why not walk and save the environment a little too (and petrol money).

- How about dusting off your bike and getting the family and your friends out on bike rides.

- Family walks are good for many things, catching up time, family together time, improving fitness, time away from chores, to see things not always seen from the car, weight management. Why not explore places near you that you have wanted to go to for ages?

- Did you know that even activities such as ironing, spring cleaning, decorating, watching comedy shows on television, talking to friends over the phone, and shopping all burn up calories?

Any new exercise or activity will help offset the weight gain you are worried about, not to mention help stave off any cravings that you might be experiencing.

Summing Up

- Whatever you change in diet or exercise habits, remember that if they are an improvement (and ideally fun) these changes will last longer.

- It's always better to do something you *want to,* rather than *have to.*

- This is the same with any lifestyle change whether it is increasing exercise, stopping smoking or having more interaction with the family.

Chapter Six

How do I Stop Smoking and Handle Stress?

Stress is one of the most common reasons for going back to smoking and it is worth going through some hints and tips around this subject to help you recognise and head off a potential return to smoking.

Cigarettes are a stimulant and increase the response to stress, often showing the same physical manifestations of stress shown overleaf.

Nicotine is highly addictive. Within seven to fifteen seconds after puffing on a cigarette, the nicotine gets to the brain and relieves the internal nagging as the body receives the nicotine it wants. This reinforces the addiction and leads to a repeat of the whole process in a few hours' or even a few days' time.

As a physical relief, smokers have said that this feeling is similar to that feeling of relief when you let go of that heavy shopping bag when you get home or you step into a warm house after walking on a freezing cold winter's day.

So, if the cigarette only relieved your physical need and has not relieved your stress, then who relieved the stress?

Did you take a break whilst you had a cigarette?

Could that have relieved your stress?

Was it the chat you had in the 'sin bin', or the mini outdoor business meeting where that good idea came from?

Could it have been the five-minute break you took?

Was it the call to the plumber to get the heating back on?

'So, if the cigarette only relieved your physical need and has not relieved your stress, then who relieved the stress?'

All these things may have been achieved whilst you had a cigarette in your hand but did the cigarette really do them all?

If the cigarette cannot fix your stress, could it have been you?

It's human nature to feel less than friendly when a colleague takes an idea of ours and then tells the boss it was their idea, yet we often let a bunch of chemicals and leaves rolled in a piece of paper take the credit for overcoming our stress instead of holding our heads up high and saying, 'I can handle my own stress from now on.'

What are the warning signs of stress?

How does my body react when I am stressed?

- Headaches.
- Dry mouth.
- Feeling weak.
- Feeling tired.
- Muscle tension.
- Pounding heartbeat.
- Increased breathing rate.
- Chest discomfort.
- Nausea.
- Heartburn.
- Aches.
- Pains.
- Twitches.
- Butterfly feeling in stomach.
- Sweating.
- Sleep problems.
- Back and neck pain.

- Pins and needles in hands and feet.

- Increased need to pass urine more frequently.

- Long-standing illnesses worsening.

How do I behave when I am stressed?

- Irritability with small things becoming bigger issues than they normally would.

- Loss of confidence.

- Becoming withdrawn or indifferent.

- Getting forgetful when your memory is normally good.

- Lack of motivation.

- Being tearful.

- Becoming unreliable when normally you are the opposite.

- Suddenly becoming obsessive (especially on time management or cleaning the oven at unusual times like 3am).

- Pushing friends away.

- Complaining more.

- Having difficulty thinking.

- Finding it hard to problem solve.

- Keeping over busy.

- Aggressive behaviour.

What can I do to relax?

Got five minutes?

- Sit down quietly (or lie down) and close your eyes for five minutes.

- Listen to your breathing and focus on slowing it down.

- Visualise cool air coming in and warm air being breathed out of your body.

※ Imagine the cares of the day being removed from your body as you breathe out.

How are the muscles?

※ Try to start noticing the feelings you get when you are stressed, such as muscle tension.

※ Try to relax your muscles by dropping your shoulders and relaxing your facial muscles.

※ Try to stop what you are doing and rest, spend time sitting quietly and breathing out the tension or distracting yourself with calming music.

※ You could try to imagine that you are somewhere else (like a warm beach). How does it feel, who are you with? Is it warm? What can you hear? Can you hear the sea crashing or children playing or the sound of leather on willow? (For cricket fans!) Having made this daydream yours, you can take yourself to this place for a few moments whenever you start to feel stressed.

Deep breathing anyone?

Three second breathing:

※ Take a deep breath.

※ Hold it for the count of three (one hundred and one, one hundred and two and one hundred and three).

※ Then slowly breathe out.

Repeat this and continue the slow breathing.

If you are comfortable you can slow to a 6 second breath by repeating the same sequence as above.

Stress, golden rules to help

This section is about how to help you tackle the thinking and behaviours that cause day-to-day stress and then give you advice on how to change those patterns and ease stress.

What else can I do?

Stress is not healthy when it gets out of control, it becomes 'distress'.

This is the term we really mean when we have reached the stage where we have had enough.

Here are some simple tips to help:

- Get priorities right. Decide what really matters and try to keep things in proportion.

- Don't set excessive goals for yourself. Being that hard on yourself usually achieves the opposite effect to success.

- Learn to delegate. Why do *you* have to do everything?

- Think ahead and try to anticipate and prevent some stressful situations from happening.

- If you are worried about your health, get help and get it sorted out before it causes you more stress.

- Share your concerns with family and friends, a problem shared is often a problem halved.

- Try to develop a social network or circle of friends, (no man is an island and we all need to have fun occasionally).

- Take regular exercise, endorphins are natural painkillers and exercise keeps you fit.

- Take regular breaks to relax during the day, stress does not build so easily then.

- Lead a fairly regular and balanced lifestyle, adapting into routines that can be helpful.

'Stress is not healthy when it gets out of control, it becomes "distress".'

- Take leisure time, relax, recharge your batteries.

- Tried soothing or motivational music?

- Try losing yourself in a book or film.

- Treat yourself occasionally for positive actions, attitudes, praise yourself when you have achieved something that means a lot to you.

- Say 'no' once in a while if you are one of those people that will always say yes and never has any time.

- Sometimes, just stop, look up and watch the birds, smell the roses, daydream. Calm quickly follows these activities.

- Get to understand yourself better, improve your own defences and strengthen your weaker points, by doing this you avoid problems.

- Think about problems realistically and decide to take the appropriate action as soon as you can or get help if you need it.

- Don't brood or bottle things up. This just makes things worse.

- Ask yourself, can I deal with the problem, do I need help or is it one of those problems that needs me to change the way I let it affect me?

- Am I being too sensitive or stubborn and is this preventing the solution to the problem from happening?

- Ask friends and family how they deal with stress.

- Whenever you can, have fun, enjoy yourself with your family and friends.

And finally:

- Understand that not all problems have solutions and sometimes you just have to say 'such is life'.

Summing Up

- Setting unreasonable, and unachievable goals, taking life, (or self), too seriously causes stress.

- Too much stress and you soon become distressed.

- Stress is easily caught and not easily cured. We lead busy lives and are always 'on the go'.

- There are many signs of stress, from headaches to chest pain, with aching limbs and stomach upsets in-between.

- Stopping and taking time to smell the roses, watch the birds in the air and the dogs bounding on the beach gives a much healthier pause in the day. As do other relaxation techniques.

- Look after yourself, understand your limits, have fun with your family and take care of your health.

- In the words of a famous song, we are told 'Don't worry, be happy'.

'Don't worry, be happy.'

Chapter Seven

Complementary Therapies

What do I mean by complementary therapies? Things like hypnosis, acupuncture and herbal remedies. Many people have successfully stopped smoking with the help of complementary therapies. Let's take a closer look.

Herbal medicine

What is herbal medicine?

Herbal medicine is also known as phytotherapy and is about using plant remedies to prevent and treat ill health.

Herbal medicine is the oldest and most universal system of medicine known and about 85% of the world's population rely on phytotherapy.

Modern Western herbal medicine is based on a combination of traditional knowledge, clinical experience, an understanding of medical sciences, and the scientific evidence base for herbal medicine, (clinical trials).

Pharmaceutical drugs have usually originated from plants where their active constituent has been specifically isolated, synthesised and then used to suppress symptoms or 'attack' disease. Herbal medicines consist of extracts of part(s) of the whole plant (roots, leaves, flowers, bark and berries). They are generally prescribed by herbalists to assist the body in healing itself.

A herbalist aims to seek and treat the underlying cause of ill health, with the treatment focusing on the individual patient and not the condition.

'Herbal medicine is the oldest and most universal system of medicine known and about 85% of the world's population rely on phytotherapy.'

Are herbalists qualified?

A qualified Western medical herbalist undertakes four years of training. This training includes the study of medical sciences, diagnostic skills, pharmacology, material medical and herbal therapeutics, as well as completing a minimum of 500 hours of supervised clinical training, to qualify with a BSc in Herbal Medicine (Phytotherapy).

Which professional organisations do they belong to?

British Herbal Medicine Association. www.bhma.info.

British Institute of Medical Herbalists/National Institute of Medical Herbalists. www.nimh.org.uk.

Members can be identified by the letters MNIMH or FNIMH and MCPP or FCPP after their name.

All members are covered by full professional insurance and adhere to a strict professional code of ethics.

Western medical herbalists use primarily British, European and North American herbs, although some Chinese herbs are also used.

Does herbal medicine help?

Medical herbalists provide a unique, personalised treatment. They often refer patients back to their GPs or consultants as the need arises.

This approach means that herbal medicine can be of benefit in treating a wide range of acute and chronic health problems in all ages, including:

- Digestive disorders. Irritable bowel syndrome, (IBS),constipation, diarrhoea, indigestion, peptic ulcer, colitis.

- Circulatory problems. High blood pressure, varicose veins and poor circulation.

- Respiratory complaints. Hay fever, asthma, sinusitis, bronchitis, coughs and colds, sore throats, recurrent infections.

- Gynaecological problems. Menopausal symptoms, period pain, PMS, irregular cycles, infertility.

- Skin conditions. Eczema, psoriasis, acne, fungal infections.

- Joint problems, arthritis, gout.

- Insomnia, depression, anxiety.

- Migraine, headaches.

- Childhood illnesses.

- Supportive treatment for chronic illness.

Bearing in mind that giving up smoking has a wide range of withdrawal and recovery effects, a herbalist can often prepare treatments that can assist you with some of the side effects.

Which herbs can help?

- Angelica. Helps with the digestive system and recovery from coughs.

- Avena. Oats can help you to give up smoking as they promote mental wellbeing (stave off 'the blues').

- Bilberry. Helps eyes and also night vision.

- Chamomile. A calming and anti-inflammatory effect.

- Cramp bark. A muscle relaxant good for period and back pains.

- Dandelion. The roots are good as a liver tonic. The leaves help you pass water easier.

- Echinacea. Helps the immune system and is good for colds.

- Elderflowers. The leaves or berries are good for colds and flu.

- Eyebright. Useful for conjunctivitis and catarrhal symptoms such as hay fever.

- Ginger. Good for nausea.

- Hawthorn. For the heart and circulation.

- Ispaghula. For constipation (Regulan and Fybogel are pharmaceutical products consisting totally of the ispaghula husk). Also helps with irritable bowel syndrome.

- Lavender. Relaxing properties, but the essential oil is also good for burns.

- Meadowsweet. Digestive complaints including heartburn.

- Nettle. A cleansing and restoring herb.

- Nutmeg. For diarrhoea and flatulent dyspepsia.

- Red Clover. For skin complaints and menopause.

- St John's wort. Good for depression, anxiety, hypertension, (high blood pressure) and tobacco withdrawal.

- Valeriana (Valerian). Helps promote sleep, relaxation and restore the nervous system.

Which conditions can herbal teas ease?

- Detoxification. Dandelion, nettle, peppermint and red clover. Cleans, refreshes and stimulates the lymphatic system and kidneys.

- Cold relief. Elderflower, peppermint and yarrow, for fever and blocked sinuses.

- Sneazeze tea. Chamomile, elderflower, eyebright, nettle and ribwort. Reduces hay fever symptoms.

- Bloatese tea. Cinnamon, fennel, ginger, lemon balm, lime flowers, and peppermint. For bloating and trapped wind.

- Perk up tea. Lemon balm, oat straw, rose petals and rosemary. A pick-me-up that repairs low energy levels and aids concentration.

- Stomach settler. Chamomile, cinnamon, meadowsweet, peppermint. Calms the digestive system.

- Pressure off tea. Hawthorn, lime flowers, yarrow. A supportive blend for the cardiovascular system.

- Calming tea. Lime flowers, peppermint, rose petals, skullcap. Relieves anxiety and tension.

- Depression and hypertension. St John's wort but take care with some medications including bupropion (Zyban).
- Lung problems. Lobelia (Indian tobacco).

Is it expensive to seek a herbalist's help?

Prices vary, but when you consider how much cigarettes are it remains cost-effective. It is unusual to access herbalist help on the NHS, as the sort of data they require from clinical trials is very expensive to obtain and so clinical trial data for consideration in large numbers is currently unavailable.

There have been a number of studies showing by experience (anecdotal evidence) that herbal medicine does help some people.

Hypnosis

Is hypnosis safe?

The British Society of Clinical Hypnosis (BSCH) is a body whose aim is to promote and assure high standards in the profession of hypnotherapy. Membership demands strict standards of training and ethical practice.

It is worth understanding what hypnotherapy is about.

The showmanship kind of hypnosis (where people run about on stage barking) is not what clinical or serious hypnotherapy is all about. Bearing in mind that hypnosis affects the psychological state of the mind, often when people are under the natural hypnotic state, their personalities, memories and experiences all affect their mental health. To interfere with just one aspect and not the other aspects that may come out when they are 'under' is extremely dangerous.

Hypnotists have assured me that despite the pre-conceived ideas that most of us have, the patients do not receive 'auto suggestion'. They are given counselling over a lengthy consultation ranging between 1½ to 2 hours, which is similar in content to many Stop Smoking advisors.

'Hypnotists have assured me that despite the pre-conceived ideas that most of us have, the patients do not receive 'auto suggestion' They are given counselling over a lengthy consultation ranging between 1½ to 2 hours, which is similar in content to many Stop Smoking advisors.'

They go through smoking beliefs, rituals and routines and the importance these have in the smoker's day. All these are decided by the patient whilst under hypnosis.

How long has hypnosis been around?

Historically, medical hypnosis has been used and accredited by the British Medical Association since the 18th century.

Many people have stated that they have benefitted from hypnotism, although currently there is no formal clinical trial data to show hypnotism is an effective therapy.

How does hypnosis work?

A hypnotic state occurs normally in everyone when certain physiological and psychological conditions are met and with the assistance of a skilled hypnotherapist it is possible to use this state to make deep and lasting changes to thoughts, feelings and behaviour.

No one can be hypnotised against their will and even when hypnotised, a person can still reject any suggestion.

When seeking a hypnotherapist, the advice is always to see someone who is affiliated and accredited to the national organisation listed in this section and ideally go to someone who has helped a friend if you choose this option.

See the help list for details on the National Register of Hypnotherapy Practitioners who can provide more information.

Acupuncture

Why acupuncture?

Acupuncture is another treatment that has seemed to help some people to stop smoking. It has also helped people with their withdrawal symptoms not just from smoking but also from other addictive substances.

Acupuncture is thought to stimulate endorphins (the body's own natural painkillers).

Acupuncture treatment claims to transform the taste of tobacco into a bad experience, which may make stopping smoking easier. This treatment can also alleviate nervousness, agitation, and other signs of mental distress.

This calming effect may also make the stopping smoking less stressful.

Which methods does an acupuncturist use to treat nicotine withdrawal?

Some use a combination of body acupuncture and the use of press-seeds on certain acupoints on your ears.

During the treatment, a needle is inserted at certain acupoints on your body. These acupoints are selected to ease the withdrawal symptoms experienced, to calm the mind, and treat the effects that smoking will have had on your lungs over the years.

If you have any other underlying problems, these would also be treated as well.

Often, special seeds are put in place on certain 'acupoints' on the ears. These are held in place by small plasters and remain in place for a few days.

Each time you experience a craving, you press the seeds to help ease the craving giving an effective treatment over the following days, and they are supposed to ease any nicotine cravings experienced.

In some areas (but not all), acupuncture treatment for pain management and other uses is becoming available within the NHS. Please refer to the help list for details of the regulators and professional organisations for acupuncture.

Laser acupuncture

A variation on acupuncture is laser therapy, which some have found useful for stopping smoking.

How does laser therapy work?

▪ It is a programme of five sessions spanning fourteen days with each lasting forty-five minutes. Ideally, three sessions must be consecutive.

▪ Laser therapy stimulates endorphins, in the same way that nicotine does, helping to suppress physical cravings and enhance willpower.

▪ As well as laser therapy you also get behavioural help and support.

▪ Blood sugar levels need to be rebalanced so they give dietary advice on how to overcome this.

▪ Treatment is not painful but you may experience a light tingly sensation, or feelings of warmth.

▪ Laser therapy has been used for the last forty years for a variety of conditions and does not burn.

Summing Up

- Some alternative therapies have been around for centuries, their effects and recipes passed from generation to generation. As symptom relief, many are as effective today as they were then with herbal remedies like ginger being recommended today to pregnant mums and varenicline users for nausea, lavender being recommended for a calming effect and St John's wort regularly recommended for anxiety and depression.

- Hypnotherapists and those who perform laser and standard acupuncture have also met with some anecdotal success over the years, both in helping people to stop smoking and relieving their withdrawal and adjustment symptoms.

- Clinical evidence in the form of trial data is somewhat sketchy and the advice is always to pick somebody who you know has treated a friend, from word of mouth recommendation or who is affiliated and registered a recognised professional organisation.

- Many people try different methods of help and it is good to remain open-minded.

'Some alternative therapies have been around for centuries, their effects and recipes passed from generation to generation. As symptom relief, many are as effective today as they were then.'

Chapter Eight

How to Support a Loved One

When someone has never smoked it is hard to understand the hold nicotine has over people they care about.

Partners and families are often at the mercy of mood swings and also have their own lives to lead. They have their own problems as well.

How many times have you heard of someone who went back to smoking because they got irritable and their relative told them to just go and have a cigarette and stop being so moody?

Could that person even have been you in the past?

Some people have returned to smoking feeling hopeless because friends or family have said to them 'What's the problem, other people *just* stop', or, 'All you need is willpower'.

Smoking is an addiction, it is hard to stop. Even ex-heroin addicts have found giving up heroin easier than stopping smoking.

The more support you have the better.

This small section will give you a few tips on how to give positive support and encouragement to your loved one towards a smoke-free life.

What can partners do to help?

- If your partner is irritable try to give the new non-smoker space. We all need space now and again.

'Smoking is an addiction, it is hard to stop. Even ex-heroin addicts have found giving up heroin easier than stopping smoking. The more support you have the better.'

- Congratulate them on how well they are doing rather than ask have they smoked. (Asking them usually reminds them that they want a cigarette.)

- Remind them that they are strong and that they can succeed, rather than the 'I knew you'd fold' brigade.

- If they do slip, remind them that they did it before so they can do it again, Rome wasn't built in a day and many people 'wobble' but eventually stop smoking.

- Buy some well done treats or arrange a trip out somewhere nice to mark the first day, week or month.

- Perhaps valet their car so that they do not want to smoke in it any more as it smells so fresh.

- How about an occasional hug if your partner is finding it tough?

- If your partner is finding it tough, how about a distraction or a quiet night in doing something you both enjoy?

- What about reminding your partner, when their resolve is a bit shaky, that it was their choice to stop and remind them of the reasons why they chose to.

- How about a bunch of flowers, a new fishing reel, a weekend in Paris?

What can friends do to help?

- Give lots of encouragement.

- Sit inside the pub with them rather than going out with the smokers (if you smoke).

- Be a listening ear when stress becomes a problem and remind your friend how strong they are and how well they are doing and how they wouldn't want to go backwards now.

- Take your friend on a smoke-free night out.

- Get pizza and beer for a friends' night in.

- Remind your friend that they chose to give up smoking because . . . (help them remember their best five reasons).

What can the children do to help?

- How about getting the children involved doing well done cards or pictures?

- Younger children love star charts (for some it is a good method of payback if they are doing one for their parents!)

- For the older children it might be asking them to make a special effort not to fight with each other, keep their rooms tidy, washing-up and helping around the place.

- How about giving them some money to buy a well done present?

- Enjoying story time and quality time together watching a film are other ways that can involve children, and both child and parent reap the benefits of a slow down in busy lives.

The possibilities are endless. Feel free to think of more.

How can I help support someone stopping when I still smoke?

- Try not to smoke around your partner.

- Avoid leaving packets of cigarettes or tobacco in reach or sight.

- Avoid asking your partner to go to the shop and pick up some cigarettes, a lighter or other such items for you, (in the early days the temptation may be too great).

- How about trying to stop smoking with them? Maybe this is the right time for you to try too? You can support each other.

Summing Up

- It is hard to stop smoking and positive support is always welcome.

- The ideas given here are not all of the ways you can help.

- The more creative you are, the more chances of helping the person you care about stay free from their addiction.

- We all need kindness, praise and a bit of fun at some time in our lives.

- Everyone benefits from a smoke-free home.

- Teamwork rules.

'Everyone benefits from a smoke-free home.'

Chapter Nine

Staying Stopped

How do I stay a non-smoker?

If you value something and life seems good with it, you will miss it when it's no longer there.

Have you decided that tobacco has no value in your life?

Are you are in control and enjoying your life without it?

In time, your routines will become more comfortable without tobacco, and generally it will be getting easier to say no.

If you do get thoughts or cravings it is worth looking back at the various sections in this book that can remind you of the principles of staying stopped and the reasons why you chose to stay smoke-free.

Have a look at the reasons why people want to end their relationship with tobacco and why some people think tobacco helps.

See where *you* are with these thoughts.

Have a lot of these reasons gone now?

Tobacco may have been in your life longer than anything else and it takes time to adjust.

Smoking is an addiction, from time to time you will get one part of your brain saying, 'Go for it. One won't hurt!' and the other part saying, 'No, don't do it. Think how hard it was to get to this point!'. These 'gremlins from within', the red or the white one, are yours, only you can train them.

'Have you decided that tobacco has no value in your life? Are you are in control and are enjoying your life without it?'

The white gremlin will need a few months' worth of training or reinforcing before it is strong enough to argue against your red one on its own in your subconscious. That's why some thoughts still seem a little stronger than others. The more you correct the thoughts of 'red gremlin', the weaker they become.

There are no easy answers and the medication has to stop some time so it is worth remembering that the medication, whether bupropion (Zyban), nicotine replacement therapy or varenicline (Champix), only catered for the physical need.

'Most people go back to smoking due to "unfinished business" either because they still like cigarettes or because they still believe there is a use for them. The more you dislike them, the less a return to smoking is likely to happen.'

The physical need gets less after three months and so is no longer needed as the nicotine receptors lie sleeping and nicotine is a near but distant memory.

Watch out though, one puff can wake them up.

The rest is up to you.

Most people go back to smoking due to 'unfinished business', either because they still like cigarettes or because they still believe there is a use for them. The more you dislike them, the less a return to smoking is likely to happen.

Be proud of what you have achieved.

You have dealt with one of the hardest addictions known to Man and have overcome most of the hardest cravings already.

Now you have completed this lifestyle change and your current challenge is achieved, how about looking for your next project?

What about stress management, weight management or an exercise regimen?

Be kind to yourself and now you have new energy perhaps you can enjoy new activities, dance classes, sports or hobbies. These will help to reinforce that you didn't need cigarettes in the first place and you are better off without.

One puff is never enough, any amount of tobacco will make you want more. Be strong and say to yourself 'not one puff'.

If you do go back to smoking, please remember that people can make several attempts to stop before they finally succeed.

Keep trying, you will get there in the end.

Help List

About.com

www.quitsmoking.about.com
Lifestyle change website offering advice on a range of subjects including stopping smoking, stress and weight management.

Action on Smoking and Health (ASH)

102 Clifton Street, London. EC2A 4HW
Tel: 020 7739 5902
www.ash.org.uk
Ash is a tobacco control lobby group that also gives a great deal of information about smoking. They have regional offices all over the UK.

Action on Smoking and Health (ASH) Scotland

www.ashscotland.org.uk
Ash (Scotland) is a tobacco control lobby group that also gives a great deal of information about smoking.

The British Acupuncture Council

63 Jeddo Road, London. W12 9HQ
Tel: 020 8735 0400
www.acupuncture.org.uk
A professional organisation striving for excellence in training, safe practice and professional conduct. They act as a regulator and supply information to the general public on the subject of acupuncture.

British Medical Acupuncture Society (BMAS)

Royal London Hospital for Integrated Medicine (formerly Royal London Homoeopathic Hospital), 60 Great Ormond St, London. WC1N 3HR
Tel: 020 7713 9437
www.medical-acupuncture.co.uk

The British Medical Acupuncture Society is a registered charity established to encourage the use and scientific understanding of acupuncture within medicine for the public benefit. It seeks to enhance the education and training of suitably qualified practitioners, and to promote high standards of working practices in acupuncture.

British Herbal Medicine Association

PO Box 583, Exeter, EX1 9GX
Tel: 08456801134
www.bhma.info
The British Herbal Medicine Association (BHMA) was founded in 1964 to advance the science and practice of herbal medicine in the United Kingdom. Also provides information on issues related to herbal medicine.

British Institute of Medical Herbalists/National Institute of Medical Herbalists

Clover House, James Court, South Street, Exeter, EX1 1EE
Tel: 01392 426022
www.nimh.org.uk
The National Institute of Medical Herbalists is a professional body and regulator representing herbal practitioners. Part of their role is training and developing their practitioners and giving information to the public.

National Register of Hypnotherapy Practitioners NRHP

First Floor, 18 Carr Road, Nelson, Lancashire, BB9 7JS
Tel 01282716839
www.nrhp.co.uk
The National Register of Hypnotherapists and Psychotherapists (NRHP) promotes the skilled use of hypno-psychotherapy by properly trained and regulated practitioners and helps anyone who is seeking treatment to find a professional, locally based hypno-psychotherapist.

NHS Choices

www.nhs.uk
A national website run by the NHS for all health information needs at all levels including health professionals.

NHS Help with Health Costs

PPC Issue Office, PO Box 854, Newcastle Upon Tyne, NE99 2DE
Tel: 0845 850 0030 (Helpline)
www.ppa.org.uk/ppa/ppcdd/patient.do
To apply for queries about pre-paid prescription cards which can save on NHS prescription costs. You can also apply by post, just complete the pre-payment certificate application form FP95, available from pharmacies and doctors' surgeries.
www.nhsbsa.nhs.uk/HealthCosts/2131.aspx

NHS National Smokers Hotline

Tel: 0800 022 4332 (helpline)
Text: Quit 8808 and give your postcode.
Facebook: www.facebook.com/nhssmokefree
www.nhs.uk/smokefree
The NHS stop smoking helpline and website giving information on stopping smoking and the services available. Offers some support by phone and online.

Nicorette 'Active Stop Programme' and iPhone app

(McNeil Healthcare (UK) Limited)
 www.nicorette.co.uk/active-stop
The programme gives support via mobile phone, a daily email, the Internet and with an iPhone app.

NiQuitin CQ, (GSK), 'Quitmasters' online interactive programme.

http://niquitin.co.uk/quit-smoking-plan/quitmasters
This programme helps you to track, target and address your moments of temptation and gives you a complete 'tailored toolkit of support, motivation and advice'.

Champix LifeRewards Programme

If you do not have access to the Internet, you can ring 0800 345 7905 (helpline), for a hard copy version of the Life Rewards Programme https://www.myliferewards.co.uk/PAGES/PxWelcome.aspx

For those who have been prescribed Champix there is the LifeRewards programme, (which is an interactive website built around daily articles and activities). You do need to have your medication package handy when subscribing online as they will want to know the batch number.

No Smoking Day

British Heart Foundation, Greater London House, 180 Hampstead Road, London, NW1 7AW
Tel: 020 7554 0142
www.nosmokingday.org.uk
A charity providing help and materials to smokers wanting to quit on No Smoking Day. Also supports health care professionals.

QUIT

Tel 0800 0022 00 (helpline)
www.quit.org.uk
A telephone support service for those wishing to stop smoking.

Book List

General Household Survey 2004

Office for National Statistics. (Available from www.ic.nhs.uk)

Smoking kills

Department of Health, A White paper on Tobacco.

Published in 1998

(available from http://www.archive.official-documents.co.uk/ document/cm41/4177/4177.htm)

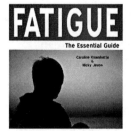